- The Colonies -

The Delaware Colony

Tamara L. Britton
ABDO Publishing Company

visit us at
www.abdopub.com

Published by ABDO Publishing Company, 4940 Viking Drive, Edina, Minnesota 55435.
Copyright © 2001 by Abdo Consulting Group, Inc. International copyrights reserved in all
countries. No part of this book may be reproduced in any form without written permission from
the publisher.

Printed in the United States.

Cover Photo Credit: North Wind Picture Archives
Interior Photo Credits: North Wind Picture Archives (pages 9, 11, 13, 15, 17, 19, 21, 25, 27, 29);
    Corbis (pages 7, 23)

Contributing Editors: Bob Italia, Kate A. Furlong, and Christine Fournier
Book Design and Graphics: Neil Klinepier

Special thanks to Jim Rementer, Project Director, Lenape Language Project, for his invaluable
assistance with this project.

Library of Congress Cataloging-in-Publication Data

Britton, Tamara L., 1963-
   The Delaware Colony / Tamara L. Britton.
      p. cm. -- (The colonies)
   Includes index.
   ISBN 1-57765-577-X
      1. Delaware--History--Colonial period, ca. 1600-1775--Juvenile literature. [1.
Delaware--History--Colonial period, ca. 1600-1775.] I. Title. II. Series.

F167 .B75 2001
975.1'02--dc21

                                                                            2001022888

Contents

The Delaware Colony

Delaware is on a narrow **peninsula**. Native Americans were the first people to settle there. Later, Swedish, Dutch, and English colonists came to Delaware.

In 1631, Dutchman David Pieterson de Vries started a Dutch colony in Delaware. Seven years later, Sweden also founded a colony there. But in 1664, England seized Delaware's land.

In Delaware, everyone worked to make the colony successful. They cleared land and built houses. Men hunted and farmed. Women took care of the home and children.

To earn money, early colonists started tobacco farms. Later industries included shipbuilding, leather tanning, and milling. Colonists traded these goods with other colonies and countries. The colony was successful.

Soon, England's king charged the colonists heavy taxes. The colonists protested. This led to the **American Revolution**.

The colonies won the war and created the United States of America. On December 7, 1787, Delaware **ratified** the U.S. **Constitution**. It became the first state of the new nation.

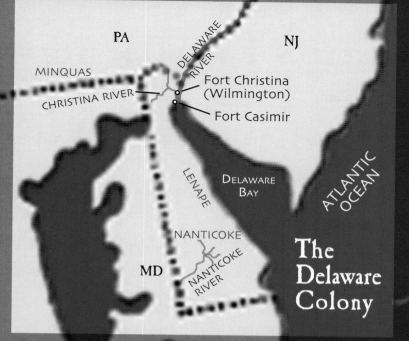

The Delaware Colony

PA

NJ

DELAWARE RIVER

MINQUAS

CHRISTINA RIVER

Fort Christina (Wilmington)

Fort Casimir

LENAPE

Delaware Bay

ATLANTIC OCEAN

NANTICOKE

NANTICOKE RIVER

MD

Detail Area

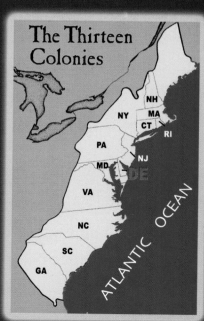

The Thirteen Colonies

NH

NY

MA

CT

RI

PA

NJ

MD

DE

VA

NC

SC

GA

ATLANTIC OCEAN

Delaware's Early History

    Delaware is located on the Atlantic Ocean. Its land is mostly a coastal plain. The sandy soil ranges from 60 feet (18 m) above sea level in the west to sea level on the Atlantic Coast.

    Delaware is on a narrow strip of land between two bays. This land is called the Delmarva **Peninsula**. Three states share the peninsula's land. Delaware is on the east, Maryland is on the west, and Virginia is on the south.

    Native Americans first lived on Delaware's land. The largest group was the Lenape (luh-NAH-pay). They spoke **Algonquian** (al-GON-kwee-an).

    The Nanticoke (NAN-tih-kohk) tribe lived along the Nanticoke River in the southwestern part of the region. The Minquas (MIN-kwahz) were a Native American tribe that lived north of Delaware, in Pennsylvania. They hunted and traded furs with Delaware's colonists.

    The Native Americans lived in villages along rivers and streams. They lived in wigwams (WIG-wahmz) made of sapling frames covered with bark. The women grew crops such as squash, beans, and corn. The men hunted and fished.

Some of Delaware's Native Americans lived along the Brandywine River.

The First Explorers

Many early explorers came to America to find new passages to China or the West Indies. In 1498, John Cabot sailed down Delaware's coast. He was exploring for England.

Then, in 1524, France sent Giovanni da Verrazzano (gee-oh-VAH-nee dah ver-rah-ZAH-noh) to America. He explored the coast from the Carolinas to Maine.

Henry Hudson explored the bay between Delaware and New Jersey in 1609. He was looking for a route to India and China for the Dutch East India Company.

Samuel Argall, a Virginia colonist, explored the same bay in 1610. He named it Delaware Bay after Virginia's governor, Thomas West Lord De La Warr.

Around 1614, Dutch explorers Cornelius May and Cornelius Hendrickson explored Delaware's land. From then until 1620, many Dutch people came to Delaware to trade. They gave Native Americans guns, cloth, and iron pots in exchange for furs.

Henry Hudson and his crew trade with Native Americans.

Delaware's First Settlements

In 1621, Dutchman William Usselinx started a trading company to make money in the New World. He hired a navigator, David Pieterson de Vries, to plan a colony.

Under de Vries's direction, Captain Peter Heyes led about 30 colonists to North America in 1631. They sailed on the ship *De Walvis*. Upon arrival, they founded a colony called Zwaanendael. In 1632, de Vries went to visit the colony. But the colony was gone.

In March 1638, Peter Minuet led Swedish colonists to North America on the ships *Kalmar Nyckel* and *Vogel Grip*. The colonists settled on the Christina River. They built a fort, and named it Fort Christina after Sweden's queen. Their settlement was called New Sweden.

In 1651, Dutchman Peter Stuyvesant founded Fort Casimir near Fort Christina. He wanted to control trade in the area. In 1654, the Swedes attacked Fort Casimir. The next year, Stuyvesant sent troops to attack New Sweden. The Dutch won and took the Swedish land. This ended Swedish rule in Delaware.

In 1664, England took over and ruled the Dutch colonies. In 1681, King Charles II gave Delaware's land to William Penn.

The next year, Penn came to Delaware. He made Delaware part of the Pennsylvania Colony. Delaware was part of Pennsylvania until 1704. Then it became a separate royal colony.

De Vries visits the remains of Zwaanendael.

Colonial Government

At Fort Christina, a council of men from the New Sweden Company governed the land. The council appointed a governor. He ruled the colony by Swedish laws. Punishments for breaking laws included fines, imprisonment, or death. Colonists had little say in the government.

In Fort Casimir, Peter Stuyvesant was the director-general. He had executive, **legislative**, and **judicial** authority over all.

In 1664, England took control of Delaware. England's King Charles II put the Duke of York in charge of Delaware. He sent a sheriff, a bailiff, and six **magistrates** to the area. They placed Delaware colonists under English laws and customs.

In 1681, King Charles II put William Penn in charge of Delaware. Delaware became part of the Pennsylvania Colony. Penn had a deputy general appointed to him. The **freemen** of the colony elected a council and assembly. The assembly could accept or reject laws, but could not propose them.

Beginning in 1701, Penn issued a new **charter**. He appointed the council and gave it executive powers. And he gave the assembly the ability to create laws. The **freemen** elected sheriffs.

In 1704, Delaware separated from Pennsylvania. It became a separate royal colony. It had its own assembly and court system. Because Delaware was a royal colony and the colonists supported the king, Delaware followed English laws.

William Penn

Life in the Colony

In Delaware, colonists worked to make their colony a success. Men ran the government. They attended the assembly meetings and voted. At home, they built houses and barns. They also worked in the fields, hunted, and butchered animals for food.

Women seldom worked away from home. They were responsible for keeping house. They milked the cows and made butter and cheese from the milk. They planted kitchen gardens. They grew peas, beans, potatoes, cabbages, beets, and pumpkins.

The women **cured** the meat that the men had butchered. They also ground corn, made clothes and soap, washed laundry, and raised the children. Women were also responsible for cooking all of their families' meals.

On Sundays, many colonists attended church. Several different religions were observed in Delaware. Swedish colonists were Lutheran. The Dutch were Dutch Reformed.

English colonists belonged to the Church of England. Other colonists were Quakers and Presbyterians (press-buh-TEER-e-unz).

Colonists grind corn by hand.

Making a Living

Delaware's early **economy** was based on farming. Swedish and Dutch colonists started tobacco farms. They also grew rye, barley, and corn. And they raised sheep and cattle.

Soon the economy expanded. Early industries included shipbuilding and leather tanning. Colonists also produced lumber and dairy products.

Colonists soon learned to use Delaware's streams and rivers. In 1787, a paper mill opened on the Brandywine River. Colonists also built flour mills there. Delaware became the center of early American flour milling.

Soon, other new businesses began in Delaware. In 1790, a textile industry began in the colony. The mills made cotton and wool products. In 1794, the Collins Forge opened. It made goods from Delaware's iron ore.

Colonists traded their goods with Native Americans and Maryland and Pennsylvania colonists. The colonists also traded with England and the West Indies.

English and Dutch colonists brought slavery to Delaware. Some of their large farms had slaves. But most farms were small and did not need many slaves.

Many Quakers thought slavery was wrong. Delaware was the only colony whose courts said all people were free until proven otherwise. Slavery existed in Delaware until the Thirteenth **Amendment** passed in 1865.

Shipbuilding was one of Delaware's first industries.

Food

Native Americans taught the colonists how to grow corn. The colonists ate corn prepared many different ways. They mixed corn and beans together to make succotash. They roasted ears of corn. And they ground corn into meal to make corn bread.

Delaware's colonists grew peas, beans, and beets in their kitchen gardens. They also grew potatoes and turnips. Apple, pear, and peach trees grew in Delaware's forests. Huckleberries, cranberries, and grapes also grew wild.

Delaware's men hunted and fished to get meat. They hunted deer, turkey, and partridge. When their farms were more successful, they raised cows and pigs.

The colonists preserved the meat for winter by packing it in salt or smoking it. They stored pumpkins and squash in cool, dry cellars. Housewives preserved and pickled all kinds of fruits and vegetables.

Cider was a popular drink in Delaware. Most colonists made their own apple cider. They drank sweet cider when the apples were first pressed. Some of the cider was stored in barrels and allowed to ferment. This made hard cider.

A farmer makes cider using a cider press.

Clothing

Early colonists had to buy their clothes from England. Later, farmers grew flax and raised sheep. Women spun flax fibers and sheep's wool on a spinning wheel to make thread. Then they wove the thread into cloth using a loom.

The women dyed the cloth different colors using plants and berries. Then they cut the cloth and sewed clothes for their families.

Women and girls wore dresses and aprons. They also wore hats that tied under the chin, called bonnets. Men wore linen shirts and **doublets**. They also wore tight-fitting pants called breeches, and kneesocks. Children wore dresses until they could walk. Then they wore the same types of clothes as their parents.

Colonists also used animal hides to make leather. They soaked the hides in **lime** and water. Then they removed animal hair and dirt. Finally, they preserved the hides by burying them in pits with bark. Then they made belts, shoes, hats, and breeches from the leather.

Peter Stuyvesant and other gentlemen wore collared shirts and breeches.

Colonial Homes

When early colonists came to America, they built houses similar to those in their homelands. The Swedish colonists built the first log cabins in America.

The one-room cabins had a large fireplace at one end. Swedish colonists made chimneys of sticks and clay. Doorways were so low that people had to stoop to enter. Swedes built a panel into the wall next to windows. They slid it over the window for protection from rain and wind.

The Dutch colonists built houses made of brick. There were plenty of bricks in the Netherlands. But when they first arrived in Delaware, there were no bricks. And there were no factories to make them. So the Dutch built **kilns** as early as 1628.

English colonists built houses of stone, brick, or wood. The most common were wood. Colonists built a timber frame and surrounded it with wood planking. The houses had one room with a thatched, pitched roof. Sometimes houses had a loft above for sleeping. A few houses were two stories tall.

This Swedish log cabin still stands at Fort Christina.

23

Delaware's Children

The people of Delaware Colony realized the importance of educating children. Swedish King Adolf Gustav II supported schools in Sweden's North American colonies. And Queen Christina allowed colonies to have as many school teachers and ministers as needed.

In 1682, William Penn's **constitution** stated that children had to learn a practical skill or trade. Many children were **apprentices**. Later, Penn said parents had to make sure their children could read by age 12.

Delaware Colony's small communities began their own schools. Usually, the community's minister taught school. Students learned in their native languages of Dutch, Swedish, and German.

Larger towns had academies. Wealthy parents sent their children to academies to prepare them for college.

Children also helped their parents with milking cows, spinning wool, and planting fields at home. When they had free time, girls and boys liked to play marbles or hopscotch. Boys also liked to go hunting or fishing.

A teacher listens to students' lessons in an early school.

Native Americans

The Lenape lived in present-day Delaware, New Jersey, and Pennsylvania. The colonists called the Lenape the Delaware because they lived near the Delaware River.

The first colonists to meet the Lenape were the Dutch. Eventually, the Lenape traded with the Dutch and Swedish colonists. In 1682, they signed a peace treaty with William Penn.

In the late 1600s, some Lenape began moving out of Delaware. They moved west into present-day Ohio.

In 1754, the French and the English fought over American land. This was called the French and Indian War. The Lenape and the Nanticoke supported the French. The English won the war in 1763. They forced most of the Native Americans out of the region.

Today, the Nanticoke and the Lenape live on **reservations** in Canada and Oklahoma. About 500 Nanticoke remain in Delaware.

The Lenape form a treaty with William Penn.

The First State

The Delaware colonists were loyal to England's King Charles II. But England passed the Stamp Act in 1765. It taxed official documents. The colonists resented the high taxes. They agreed not to import goods that needed a stamp.

In 1773, the Bostonians held the Boston Tea Party. They dumped tea in the harbor to protest England's taxes. In return, England closed Boston's port. Delaware colonists raised money to help the people of Boston. Then, Delaware sent delegates to the **Continental** Congress in 1774.

On July 4, 1776, the colonies declared independence from England. And in September 1776, Delaware adopted a state **constitution**. All the colonies worked together to defeat the English in the **American Revolution**.

The Delaware Regiment fought in the Continental Army. On Christmas night, 1776, they crossed the Delaware River to support George Washington's troops in the Battle of Trenton.

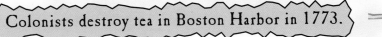

Colonists destroy tea in Boston Harbor in 1773.

There was one battle of the **American Revolution** fought in Delaware. It was the Battle of Cooch's Bridge, fought on September 3, 1777. Afterwards, the English occupied Wilmington for one month.

Colonists won the war in 1783. On December 7, 1787, Delaware **ratified** the U.S. **Constitution**. It became the first state of the new nation.

Today, Delaware is the second smallest state in America. Chemical production is its most important industry. Delaware's historic attractions bring many visitors to the state.

TIMELINE

1498 - John Cabot sails down Delaware's coast
1524 - Giovanni da Verrazzano explores Delaware's coast
1609 - Henry Hudson explores Delaware Bay
1610 - Samuel Argall explores and names Delaware Bay
1614 - Dutch explorers visit Delaware's land; begin trade with the Native Americans
1631 - Peter Heyes founds Dutch colony in Delaware
1638 - Peter Minuet founds Swedish colony in Delaware; builds Fort Christina
1651 - Dutchman Peter Stuyvesant founds Fort Casimir
1654 - Swedes take control of Fort Casimir
1655 - Dutch regain control of Fort Casimir and take over Swedish colony
1664 - England takes Delaware's land from the Dutch
1681 - King Charles II gives Delaware's land to William Penn
1682 - Delaware becomes part of the Pennsylvania Colony; Lenape sign peace treaty with William Penn
1704 - Delaware becomes a royal colony
1754 - French and Indian War begins; ends nine years later
1765 - Stamp Act passes
1773 - Boston Tea Party
1774 - Delaware sends delegates to the Continental Congress
1776 - Colonies declare independence from England; Delaware adopts a state constitution
1777 - Battle of Cooch's Bridge; English troops occupy Wilmington
1787 - Delaware ratifies the U.S. Constitution

Glossary

Algonquian - a family of Native American languages spoken from Labrador, Canada, to the Carolinas and westward into the Great Plains.

Amendment - a change to the U.S. Constitution.

American Revolution - 1775-1783. A war between England and its colonies in America. The colonists won their independence and created the United States.

apprentice - a person who learns a trade from a skilled worker.

charter - a written contract that states a colony's boundaries and form of government.

constitution - the laws that govern a state or country.

Continental - of or relating to the North American colonies.

cure - to prepare meat so that it can be eaten several months later.

doublet - a close-fitting jacket worn by men.

economy - the way a colony uses its money, goods, and natural resources.

freeman - a man free from bondage or slavery. A freeman often owned land and had the right to vote for assembly members.

judicial - related to the branch of government that controls the law.

kiln - an oven, furnace, or heated area used to process a substance.

legislative - the branch of government that makes the law.

lime - a white substance that comes from limestone, shells, or bone.

magistrate - an officer in government who can apply and enforce the law.

peninsula - land almost completely surrounded by water but connected to a larger land mass.

ratify - to officially approve.

reservation - land set aside by the government for Native Americans to live on.

Web Sites

The Swedish Colonial Society http://www.colonialswedes.org
Learn more about the history of New Sweden on this site. Or, look at some of Delaware's unique historic sites.

Delaware Tribe of Indians http://www.delawaretribeofindians.nsn.us/
Learn more about Delaware's Native Americans, the Lenape. This site has information about Lenape clothing, dances, history, and games.

These sites are subject to change. Go to your favorite search engine and type in Delaware Colony for more sites.

Index